SHAWN MENDES

ULTIMATE FAN BOOK

MALCOLM CROFT

CARLTON
BOOKS

INTRODUCTION

"I'M PROUD TO SAY I'M A ROLE MODEL."
SHAWN MENDES

2016 is the year when Shawn Mendes became the megastar he deserves to be. He recorded his first, six-second Vine video in his bedroom, and since then has ascended to the role of the cool Prince of Pop in just three years. His highly praised second album, *Illuminate*, was released in September 2016 and showcases an amazing blend of melody, maturity and musicianship. It is the singer's defining achievement so far. The sky is no longer the limit for the multitalented star, who is currently bursting through the clouds toward world domination.

This ultimate fan book is your VIP backstage pass into Shawn's unbelievable life, something to hold and cuddle while listening to his awesome music, just in case you never get the chance to cuddle the real thing. But never say never: dreams can come true – just ask Shawn!

This was an early photo shoot for Shawn, at the start of his career, aged 15.

NO PLACE LIKE HOME

HE'S SIX-FOOT-TWO TALL, HAS DARK BROWN HAIR, A FAMOUS QUIFF AND A SMILE THAT GOES ON FOR MILES AND MILES, AND HE TRAVELS THE WORLD PLAYING GUITAR. HAVE YOU SEEN ANYONE MATCHING THIS DESCRIPTION LATELY? IF YOU HAVE, CHANCES ARE IT'S SHAWN MENDES, THE HOTTEST SOLO ACT IN THE WORLD RIGHT NOW!

Shawn Peter Raul Mendes was born on 8 August 1998, and he's since made his parents, Karen and Manuel Mendes, supremely proud. Shawn's family, including his younger sister Aaliyah, live happily in the picturesque suburb of Pickering, a small, sleepy and often (says Shawn) "suffocating" town in Toronto, in the province of Ontario in Canada. With a population of just 100,000 people – and not a lot to keep a young and curious mind entertained – Pickering was just the inspiration Shawn needed to become who he truly is. "Posting songs online became a fun thing to do after school in a boring town," he has said. "With the life I live and always moving, Pickering is a little suffocating at times, but it's also the most comforting place in the world. It's nice to go back there."

When life on the road isn't sending Shawn off to far-flung locations, and when his world tours, award shows and album promos come to a crunching stop, Shawn flies home to a "normal, average" life in Pickering. It's where his heart is. But it's also what has made him search to achieve more. "Growing up in a suburban home the world seems so massive to you. It seems like cities are so big and so far away and there's so much in them. So your imagination runs

Right Shawn speaks at SiriusXM Studios in New York to promote his new EP, July 22, 2014.

Opposite The Royal Canadian Mounted Police escort Shawn to the Juno Awards, Canada, March 15, 2015.

wild." Like so many prodigious talents, the restraints of suburbia have offered inspiration, his accomplishments are born from humble beginnings. "We are an average family with an average house," said Shawn. "And I am just your average kind of guy. My parents are proud of me, but at the same time, we have trouble fathoming everything that's happened. It's crazy."

Shawn's success online with Vine was born out of his daily frustration at Pine Ridge secondary school in Toronto. "I was an average student, I wasn't any standout," he recalled. A fan of ice hockey and football, Shawn enjoyed his classes at school, but "loved entertainment and acting, performing, the stage and having the spotlight and stuff" more than studying. He is currently finishing high school online, amid all of his touring and recording commitments. Andrew Gertler, Shawn's manager and the Island Records man-with-a-plan who discovered Shawn one fateful night, once offered a poignant insight into his protégée's school years. "Shawn always tells me that early on, when he was starting to sing and starting to post covers – and this was before anything happened and before anything went viral – he would go to school and people would make fun of him. But he had his core group of friends and his family who had his back." Of course, now that Shawn is famous, no one makes fun of

SHAWN'S HOME PLAYLIST

'WHY GEORGIA' – JOHN MAYER

'LOVE YOURSELF' – JUSTIN BIEBER

'MOVE TOGETHER' – JAMES BAY

'HEY THERE DELILAH' – PLAIN WHITE T'S

'THINKING OUT LOUD' – ED SHEERAN

'HERE' – ALESSIA CARA

'THAT SWEATER' – SCOTT HELMAN

'ONE AND ONLY' – ADELE

'APOLOGIZE' – ONEREPUBLIC

him for his Vine videos. In three short years, Shawn has gone from bored teenager to bedroom superstar to No.1 sensation.

Unlike his own idols, Shawn has achieved all this without a headline-grabbing bad-boy attitude ("I've never had a scandal, but I don't know if that's so much because

This page Shawn performs at Austin Mahone's tour date in Washington on August 4, 2014.

Opposite above The Mendes Army awaits as Shawn leaves a taping of the popular US morning talk show *Live With Kelly And Michael*, July 24, 2014.

Opposite below Shawn poses for a "Shawnie" or "Shawn Selfie" with a fan at the 2014 US Open in New York.

I'm perfect, or because people aren't caring enough yet"). For Shawn his small-town charm, melodic songs and lovable face are enough. "I remember when people started to know who I was and the label offers came in, people started to get a little weird and be weird around me," Shawn recalled. "But now when I go back, people are fine. The people I'm surrounded by are really awesome people, and are really heart-to-heart with me. A lot of it comes down to my family and people I hang out with, my friends not acting any different when I come home. My parents being really awesome. I really love going back home. I think going back to a nice, relaxed little town is the best way to do it." For many of his fans, Shawn Mendes is the Clark Kent of the pop universe: a small-town boy at home, a superhero pop star to the rest of the world.

> "MY DAD ALWAYS SAYS THAT I'M A TORTURED SOUL BECAUSE I'M NEVER PLEASED. I NEVER FEEL LIKE I DESERVE WHAT I'VE ACHIEVED."
>
> *SHAWN MENDES*

THE START OF SOMETHING BIG

WITH ONE OF SHAWN'S PERSONAL IDOLS, ED SHEERAN, TAKING A BREAK FROM MUSIC SINCE 2015, THERE IS A HUGE GAP IN THE MALE POP UNIVERSE THAT NEEDS FILLING. A SUPER-TALENTED, MULTI-INSTRUMENTALIST WITH A NICE FACE – SHAWN PERFECTLY FITS THE BILL, DON'T YOU THINK?

Shawn, the "most average kid ever", began posting a string of six-second covers by One Direction, 5 Seconds of Summer, Justin Bieber and many others on the quick-hit, video-sharing platform Vine in 2013. He had only learned to play the guitar six months before: "I think I was just bored one summer afternoon," he recalled in an interview to his hometown newspaper, "and I decided to post a little video of me singing and playing guitar out of tune." This "moment of spontaneity", as he called it, would go on to change his life forever. "Singing kind of came out of nowhere, and I was pretty bad at first," Shawn has said of the mysterious origin of his talent. "I would say I didn't start getting very good at singing until last year!" We don't believe you, Shawn!

"I promise you, if you look at YouTube and see some of my first covers, you will hear that I don't sound good. But I was so obsessed with it and wanted so much to be good at it that I forced myself to figure out what sounds right and what sounds wrong," Shawn recalled. In a matter of months, Shawn quickly saw the rise of more than 200,000 loyal and lovable followers, now famously known as the Mendes Army. By August 2014, Shawn's quest for perfection helped him become the third most-followed musician on Vine. His hashtag – #shirtlessshawn, inspired by a series of selfies showing off his toned abs – has helped him too, for obvious reasons!

With Shawn's not-quite pitch-perfect covers making waves online it was only a matter of time before he would be discovered. His big break came in 2014, when artist manager Andrew Gertler typed the words "Say Something" into Google, a song he had just heard on *The Voice*. Shawn's cover of the song was the first result that popped up. Andrew clicked the link. "You see a lot of YouTube artists who spend a lot of time on a good edit, and it almost feels fake or manufactured," remembered Andrew, now Shawn's manager, in an interview. "But Shawn's voice was so good, so different from every other person you see posting covers.

"I WAS SUPER-OBSESSED WITH COVER VIDEOS. WHEN I WAS 10, I WOULD COME HOME FROM SCHOOL AND WATCH THEM FROM 4PM UNTIL 8PM EVERY NIGHT. I WAS SO INTRIGUED THAT PEOPLE TOOK THESE SUPER-POPULAR SONGS AND DID THEM THEIR OWN WAY." *SHAWN MENDES*

Opposite Singer. Guitarist. Hottie. Shawn performs at Z100's Jingle Ball 2014 pre-show at Hammerstein Ballroom, New York, December 12, 2014.

Above Shawn arrives to tape his first ever appearance on the *Late Show with David Letterman*, November 13, 2014.

The other amazing thing was how fast he was gaining views and followers. He would tweet, 'I want pizza,' and it would get 30,000 favourites! He had way fewer followers than some other artists, but he was *connecting*."

However, in order to become a superstar, Shawn needed a hit song of his own: a debut single that would break through the noise and announce his arrival to the world. Released in June 2014 as the lead track of *The Shawn Mendes EP*, the aptly named 'Life of the Party' was the perfect choice. Shawn became deeply connected to the track lyrically and musically, and the title sums up everything we've now come to know and love about our new favourite artist. *The Shawn Mendes EP* was released on 28 July 2014, and to the surprise of Shawn and many people in the music industry, it reached No.1. on iTunes – in just 37 minutes! The EP earned Shawn the title of the youngest person to debut in the top 25 on the *Billboard Hot 100*. He was just 15 years, 11 months and four days of age.

The party was starting and Shawn was on his way...

HEARD IT ON THE GREAT VINE

HIS FELLOW SOCIAL MEDIA STARS, SUCH AS JUSTIN BIEBER, GREYSON CHANCE, 5 SECONDS OF SUMMER AND AUSTIN MAHONE GOT THEIR BIG BREAK ON YOUTUBE. SHAWN MENDES, CANADIAN PIN-UP AND PRINCE OF BLUES-POP, WAS THE FIRST STAR TO BLOSSOM ON VINE.

The social media app Vine may now have withered and died, but in its brief time online it propelled Shawn on to the world's pop stage, where he belongs. Shawn's fans first stumbled on to him when he began using Vine, uploading videos that were only seconds long – but that's all the time this musical prodigy needed for fans to realize his true potential.

After uploading a clip of himself playing guitar and singing an acoustic version of Justin Bieber's 'As Long As You Love Me', Shawn's following skyrocketed. Overnight, it received more than 10,000 likes! Within months of being an active poster, Shawn had a following of hundreds of thousands of subscribers, as well as millions of views on each of his videos. The teen heart-throb has now gone on to achieve more than five million followers on Vine, 7.5 million on Twitter and more than four million likes on Facebook.

"Social media is everything," Shawn has said in an interview. "I wouldn't have anything without social media. My whole career revolves around that for sure. Just being yourself, keeping your fans updated, stay active and keeping in touch with them. I am being myself, it's how I'd do it naturally. I was consistent with these six-second videos of me singing on YouTube, on Twitter, on Instagram. I was posting pictures all the time. I didn't know what I was doing, but I was doing something!"

Since 2013, Shawn has been catapulted into the spotlight after signing with Island Records and releasing a No.1 EP and two mega-selling albums, *Handwritten* in 2015 and *Illuminate* in 2016. In October 2016, Shawn sold out New York's Madison Square Garden in less than five minutes. He has more than one billion views on YouTube, more than eight million fans on Twitter and many

Opposite Shawn signs autographs for his fans at Boston Children's Hospital, November 14, 2014.

This page Shawn sings 'Life of the Party' for 20,000 Canadian students at Rogers Arena, October 22, 2014.

Opposite Fans with phones aloft at Hot 99.5's Jingle Ball 2014, December 15, 2014.

Above Shawn, Ryan Seacrest and Usher attend a special event in honour of Boston Children's Hospital, November 14, 2014.

Right Armed with his trusty acoustic, Shawn performs solo at the We Day Vancouver event, Rogers Arena, October 22, 2014.

THE SHAWN MENDES EP

1. 'LIFE OF THE PARTY'
2. 'SHOW YOU'
3. 'ONE OF THOSE NIGHTS'
4. 'THE WEIGHT'

celebrity friends who think he's the most charming dude they've ever met. Shawn achieved all of this *before* his nineteenth birthday. However, age means nothing to him: "Because I'm young, obviously, a lot of people say 'Wow, his music is so mature," Shawn said in an interview. He commented, "My age gets brought up a lot," but he also explained, "I think no one should be judged on their age. Age is just a number. People start judging you on how young you are immediately before they even get to know you."

Ever since Shawn broke through on Vine, the only thing that has mattered to him is the hard work he puts into making his music. This hard work has paid off – something big!

"Ed Sheeran has been my work mother, he always gives me advice. He was the first person to tell me to work my ass off. He said if you want to be successful, then you have to work when people are sleeping and say yes to everything. So that's what I'm doing, I want to get to the top."

But it wasn't just Ed's hard work that inspired him. Taylor Swift also played an important part in influencing the young singer's superstar status. It is her down-to-earth attitude that Shawn is in awe of – and is inspired by. "With Taylor, the biggest thing I learned, and I love to say it, is that there's no amount of success that stops you from working hard," Shawn stated. "I'm pretty sure she's probably the epitome of what a music star can be. She's the coolest person ever, honestly. She's Taylor Swift, the most popular celebrity in the world, and you would never know it, she's so humble, and so down to earth."

With the support of the loyal Mendes Army behind him, Shawn's hard work and ambition to be the greatest pop star, but also just a good guy, is now within his grasp. All he has to do is hold on. It's going to be a wild ride!

Right Shawn and his band make the 2015 Much Music Video Awards extra special, June 21, 2015.

"I USED TO SPEND HOURS AND HOURS MAKING VINES, AND I WORKED SO HARD TO GET HERE. I WAS ALWAYS ONLINE. I WAS ONE OF THOSE KIDS WHO WAS JUST ALWAYS ON THE INTERNET, ALWAYS ON YOUTUBE, SO IT WAS EASY FOR ME TO DO IT. IT'S NOT WORK. IT'S JUST FUN." *SHAWN MENDES*

SHAWN'S LIFE IN NUMBERS

1. *Illuminate* reached No.**1** in the *Billboard* charts in the USA and Canada in September 2016
2. In 2017, Shawn will perform **22** dates in the USA and two in Canada as part of his 45-date world tour
3. Shawn was discovered on Vine and became the **third** most-followed musician on Vine by August 2014.
4. In July 2014, Shawn's **four**-track debut EP, *The Shawn Mendes EP*, reached No.1 on iTunes in 37 minutes!
5. In 2016, Shawn has more than **five** million likes on Facebook and more than 4.8 million followers on Vine
6. In 2013, Shawn became famous for his **six**-second snippets of popular songs and gained millions of followers in a few months
7. Shawn now has more than **seven** million fans on Twitter and 6.5 million Vevo subscribers. Shawn's music videos have had 1.5 billion views on YouTube and he has a global social media presence with 14.2 million followers on Instagram
8. Shawn was born on **8** August 1998
9. *Handwritten*'s running time is 3**9** minutes 2**9** seconds
10. The official music video for Shawn's first single, 'Life of the Party', premiered on **10** March 2015

HANDWRITTEN IN THE STARS

IN THE PAST FEW YEARS, THE WORLD OF POP HAS BEEN BLOWN TO SMITHEREENS BY FEMALE MONONYMS SUCH AS ADELE, RIHANNA, BEYONCÉ, MILEY, SELENA, ARIANA, KATY, DEMI, TAYLOR – ALL OF WHOM HAVE SHATTERED WORLD RECORDS. BUT NOW THERE'S A NEW BOY ON THE BLOCK…

Below The 2015 JUNO Awards, March 15, saw Shawn wow the crowd.

Opposite above Greeting extra lucky fans with an awesome performance the day *Handwritten* hits the shops at Minnesota's Mall of America, April 13, 2015.

Opposite below Shawn puts his selfie stick to good use for *Good Morning America*, April 17, 2015.

Don't let Shawn's handsome and baby-faced looks fool you: the singer is wise and mature beyond his teenage years. With a square jaw that could chisel diamonds and large brown eyes that act like tractor beams, it's no surprise that the singer-songwriter is making waves, not only as the biggest songwriting talent of 2016, but also as a sex symbol for his millions of fans – girls and boys of all ages. Between the release of his debut album *Handwritten* in 2015 and *Illuminate* in 2016, Shawn has been busy being a rising star, but his songs have helped him keep his feet firmly on the ground.

The success of *Handwritten* made Shawn the youngest artist since Justin Bieber to have a No.1 album. It was a lot of pressure for someone still so young, Imagine being No.1 at 16! "This is all happening so fast," Shawn admitted in an interview in 2015. "A few months ago I wasn't this popular and people didn't know about my music, and now all of the sudden there are screaming girls down the block. They're singing my songs live. It's unbelievable."

For *Handwritten*, Shawn knew that in order to be more than just a "teenage artist", he had to write his own songs. He had to be credible. "Ed Sheeran wrote his songs, so I wanted to write my own songs," Shawn recalled.

"I was just really eager and really excited to make music," Shawn remembers of his debut album's recording. His manager, Andrew Gertler, agreed: "Shawn had written a bunch of songs on his own. From the very beginning, he was set on the fact that he was going to write his own music and that he was a songwriter. When we heard some of these songs, everyone's ears perked up. He was so naturally talented."

SHAWN MENDES

HANDWRITTEN TRACKS

1. 'LIFE OF THE PARTY'
2. 'STITCHES'
3. 'NEVER BE ALONE'
4. 'KID IN LOVE'
5. 'I DON'T EVEN KNOW YOUR NAME'
6. 'SOMETHING BIG'
7. 'STRINGS'
8. 'AFTERTASTE'
9. 'AIR' (FEATURING ASTRID S)
10. 'CRAZY'
11. 'A LITTLE TOO MUCH'
12. 'THIS IS WHAT IT TAKES'

The super-melodic beauty of 'Stitches' or the sweetness of 'Never Be Alone', made Shawn's own brand of songwriting stand out. "I wouldn't write about what I don't believe in. I'm just writing about what I'm going through. My fans are growing with me and most of them are my age. It's an awesome thing because I know that we're all going through the same stuff. We're all of the same age, same generation. I'm not just writing songs that are narrating my life, but everyone else around my age because they're super-relatable."

A helping hand from established songwriters such as Ido Zmishlany, Scott Harris, Geoffrey Warburton and Teddy Geiger, helped the album to sail to to No.1 on the *Billboard* 200, selling 119,000 album-equivalent units in its first week! Not bad for a teenager from Pickering.

The album's success caught the attention of Taylor Swift, who swiftly signed Shawn up as a support act on her 1989 tour. It was the perfect match... and it gave Shawn even more encouragement to work harder for his fans, and his career.

"I learned a lot when I supported Taylor Swift during her world tour in 2015," Shawn remembered. "She never stopped working... Even the people at the top of the food chain are putting in countless hours." When you're the new Prince of Pop, touring with the Queen of Pop and seeing all the chaos up close offers a real learning curve. Shawn learned in particular how to cope with his new-found fame. "I'm intimidated by Taylor Swift. Not in a bad way, but I see her and I'm like: 'OMG, what do I do? What do I say?' So I understand how people might feel meeting me!"

Above Shawn performs 'Stitches' at Toronto's Much Music Video Awards, June 21, 2015.

SHAWN'S TOP 10 TWEETS 2016

1. "Waking up every day looking more and more like my dad, ha ha. I don't hate it."
2. "A bit home sick, ready to see my friends and family."
3. "So unbelievably grateful for everything guys, thank you so much."
4. "Getting really tired of this not sleeping thing! No pun intended! Ha."
5. "DO WHAT MAKES YOU SMILE! That's all."
6. "The quickest way to happiness, learn to be selfless."
7. "I've got the greatest band in the world. So lucky to have these guys."
8. "So unreal guys we are No.1 in over 60 countries, can't believe this you are incredible!!!"
9. "I hope you love *Illuminate*. Thank you for giving me inspiration to create something that I'll keep with me for a life time."
10. "On the roof of my hotel looking at Manhattan from afar and I feel like I'm on top of the world. Thank you guys so much."

MAKING ILLUMINATE

THE SUCCESS OF *HANDWRITTEN* WAS WRITTEN IN THE STARS. THE TOUR WITH TAYLOR SWIFT WAS THE PERFECT COMBINATION OF POP ROYALTY AND IT PROPELLED SHAWN INTO THE STRATOSPHERE. MODELLING CONTRACTS, AWARDS AND MILLIONS OF FANS JOINING SHAWN ON HIS JOURNEY WERE ALL BUT ASSURED. BUT, LIKE ALL GREAT ARTISTS, THERE WAS ONLY ONE THING ON SHAWN MENDES' MIND IN 2016 – A NEW ALBUM: SOMETHING BIG THAT WOULD TRULY DEFINE HIM.

This page Shawn's starry-eyed splendour, iHeartRadio Music Awards Fan Army Nominee Celebration, March 27, 2015.

Opposite above Shawn gives thanks to his Mendes Army during the Teen Choice Awards 2015, August 16, 2015.

Opposite below Shawn and Mauro Castano from *Cake Boss* are the life of the party at the Island Records 2015 Holiday Party, December 11, 2015.

On 5 October 2015, after much speculation about the two stars in the music press, Shawn Mendes received a tweet from fellow Canadian superstar Justin Bieber. @Justinbieber wrote:

"Shawn Mendes' voice makes me smile. Truly a gift to be able to move people's emotions through songs! So proud of you brother! Great album!"

The nod from JB made Shawn's day. It was confirmation of Shawn's meteoric rise to the top: the King was now handing down the reins to the new Prince. But before the release of the "difficult second" album in September 2016, Shawn and his team had a lot of work to do in order to hit the same heights as *Handwritten*. It wasn't going to be an easy, or fun, recording process. Or was it?

"We went up to this place called the Club House in upstate New York, in the middle of the woods," Shawn remembered in an interview. "It was the most beautiful area on this massive hill, and we'd just do whatever we wanted, for a week. And as long as we were writing music, we were being productive. We just did whatever we wanted, which was so fun for me. It was such a freeing experience."

It was this creative environment that allowed Shawn to remember that fame should not be taken seriously or for granted - that only the songs should be taken seriously and only the songs matter.

"The writing process for *Illuminate* was probably one of the most memorable processes of my life," Shawn recounted on the record. "We're all laying on the floor in the studio just looking at the ceiling, and just writing. Just talking about everything. The good thing about me and the people I worked with and wrote the album with, is that we're all extremely close friends. So, half the time we were writing, half the time we were just talking and hanging out, and that's I think what made the songs so special."

Opposite Performing at Miami's Y-100 radio station, April 7, 2015.

This page Backstage mayhem and mess at Nickelodeon's 28th Annual Kids' Choice Awards, March 28, 2015.

MUSIC VIDEOS: TOP 10

What's your favourite music video?

1. "TREAT YOU BETTER"
2. "MERCY"
3. "STITCHES"
4. "SOMETHING BIG"
5. "RUIN"
6. "I KNOW WHAT YOU DID LAST SUMMER"
7. "AFTERTASTE"
8. "LIFE OF THE PARTY"
9. "NEVER BE ALONE"
10. "A LITTLE TOO MUCH"

But which one has been been viewed the most on YouTube?

This closeness to his collaborators is the X factor that makes Shawn so in demand. When you're the Mr Nice guy of pop, everybody wants to work with you. And Shawn believes this is the secret sauce to the album's success: "If you could picture a bunch of grown men at camp, it was literally the most stress-free, do-what-you-will environment. It was like we left the earth for 10 days and were on some other planet."

The recording of *Illuminate* may have been pure fun in the woods, but the lyrical themes expressed by both Shawn and the songwriters are both poignant and reflective. The title itself serves as a reminder that music should always shed a healing light on people during their darkest hours. "It's a little dark," Shawn admitted about the title. "But when people are going through rough times in their life, music is kind of the biggest thing that sheds light on people through their dark times. And that was kind of where we were coming from."

The differences between Shawn's first and second albums also serve as reminder of just how much Shawn has grown up in three years. He was now a man, no longer a boy. "From 15 to 18, everybody is a different person," he said. "There's just so much happening to me right now." Shawn's maturity was also apparent on the new record.

"Fans might be surprised by some of the content in some of the songs. It's a lot more mature. What I'm talking about is a bit more grown up, so I think maybe they'll be surprised by some of that.

> ## "I COULD NEVER CHOOSE A FAVOURITE SONG, BUT PERSONALLY, 'UNDERSTAND' IS THE SONG THAT IS PROBABLY THE MOST PERSONAL TO ME. IT'S A LOT ABOUT GROWING UP, AND MY FRIENDS, AND JUST FEELINGS AND EMOTIONS ALL POURED INTO ONE SONG." *SHAWN MENDES*

When I wrote *Handwritten*, I was 15. And when I wrote *Illuminate*, I was 17/18. So not only do you change a lot in that time, just as a person, but when you're in this crazy world, a lot changes. You have a lot to write about. It's such a difference: vocally, lyrically. The songs are so much better. I love *Handwritten* but I really love *Illuminate*. It's so much better to me."

It was Shawn's maturity that also shone through on his desire to have total control of his music: "In terms of the production, I knew that not only did I want to be a part of writing every single song, I wanted to make sure the production and every aspect of the song was completely from my mind and heart, so I was there right beside the producer throughout it all. If I'm not in control, I feel the whole world is about to collapse." It was this desire for control of his sound and songs that shows Shawn's growth as an artist, but also as a true troubadour and spokesperson for the emotive and passionate millennial generation: "As an 18-year-old guy, to go and write an entire album that's the majority about love, people would be scared to do it. But I think it's beautiful..." So do we, Shawn. So do we.

THE LIGHT OF A NEW STAR

WITH HIS SECOND ALBUM, *ILLUMINATE*, RELEASED IN SEPTEMBER 2016 AND HITTING THE NO.1 SPOT ON THE DAY OF ITS RELEASE, SHAWN WAS NO LONGER IN DANGER OF BEING A ONE-HIT WONDER. SHAWN, THE MEGASTAR OF MELODIC POP AND ACOUSTIC BLUES-ROCK, HAD ARRIVED. AND THE PARTY WAS JUST BEGINNING TO HEAT UP.

This page Shawn gets up close and personal with fans at KIIS FM's Jingle Ball on December 4, 2015.

Opposite Strike a pose! Shawn in the NBC photo booth during the 2015 iHeartRadio Music Awards, March 29, 2015.

Following hot on the heels of *Handwritten*, which debuted at No.1 on *Billboard 200* in April 2015 and prompted *Time* magazine to include him in their "25 Most Influential Teens" list, *Illuminate* also smashed into the charts in first place, outselling many of Shawn's contemporaries, and even one or two of his idols. But this new fame, wealth and success all paled in comparison to one experience most could only ever dream of: being serenaded to by Taylor Swift on his eighteenth birthday!

For Shawn Mendes, dreams were coming true almost every day. But with superstardom, comes anxiety, as every true artist understands. "Last night I was onstage thinking, 'I'm a rock star'," recalled Shawn in an interview. "I've never been so happy and excited and at the top of wherever I could be, on cloud nine. But I've also never been so deep in the ground – thinking, 'I can't breathe', in my entire life. The greatest artists are tortured souls. I'm not calling myself great. I'm tortured because I care. I'm always upset about not

TRACKS OF MY TEARS

What's your favourite Illuminate track?

1. 'RUIN'
2. 'MERCY'
3. 'TREAT YOU BETTER'
4. 'THREE EMPTY WORDS'
5. 'DON'T BE A FOOL'
6. 'LIKE THIS'
7. 'NO PROMISES'
8. 'LIGHTS ON'
9. 'HONEST'
10. 'PATIENCE'
11. 'BAD REPUTATION'
12. 'UNDERSTAND'

Opposite Shawn Mendes and Hailee Steinfeld cuddle up at the 2015 American Music Awards, November 22, 2015.

Above Shawn Mendes and his band light up the stage, and bring in the New Year at Pitbull's Revolution 2016, December 31, 2015.

doing things as good as I think I could have... because I care."

After the release of *Illuminate*, Shawn was determined to stay true to himself, his vision and his music. He swiftly worked out that the stress of success can take its toll, and that the rollercoaster of fame has its ups *and* downs. "I've gotten off the road and been like, 'I hate singing, I hate playing guitar.' However, six days later I'm in my bedroom singing at the top of my lungs because... I love it so much."

With all of the songs on *Illuminate* written by Shawn, in collaboration with songwriter Scott Harris, producer Jake Gosling, and artists Teddy Geiger and Geoff Warburton, the curse of the "difficult second album" never appeared, and the album turned out even better than Shawn had ever hoped for. He had found his voice, his groove and his confidence, following the success of *Handwritten*. All he had to do was believe in himself.

"I'm way more confident with this album. I just feel so good about it," he reported in a 2016 interview. "If it sold no records, I'd still be

so much more confident. I'm so passionate about the music I created that, if it sold 10 copies the first day, I'd still be happy. You put a lot of effort into it – your heart, your soul. Everything goes into that album that you've been working on for the past year. So no matter what, it's a big thing."

Shawn's achievement on *Illuminate* sprang from his natural talent: he is a songwriter who can convey a wide range of subjects and emotions within his songs. "Writing love songs is easy," he has said. "Writing the songs that are about life and the things that actually happen to you is the hard part. It's hard to dig into that second part of your brain and be like, 'What happened to me? What's really affected me, either in a bad way or a good way?' And then, let's write about it."

With *Illuminate*'s success confirmed by multi-platinum sales all over the globe, all ears will be on what music the singer records next. But for now, Shawn is rightly enjoying the afterglow of his own illumination.

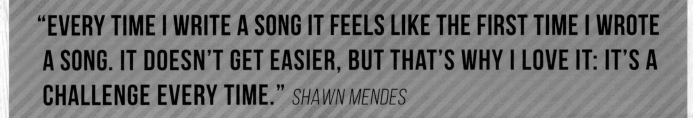

"EVERY TIME I WRITE A SONG IT FEELS LIKE THE FIRST TIME I WROTE A SONG. IT DOESN'T GET EASIER, BUT THAT'S WHY I LOVE IT: IT'S A CHALLENGE EVERY TIME." *SHAWN MENDES*

"WE WANT SHAWN, WE WANT SHAWN!"

A SELF-PROCLAIMED "EARLY BIRD", SHAWN MAY HAVE TO ADAPT HIS 9.30AM MORNING WORKOUT ROUTINE DURING HIS 2017 ILLUMINATE WORLD TOUR. LATE NIGHTS, LOUD FANS AND TOURING THE ARENAS OF THE WORLD IS UP NEXT ON SHAWN'S ROUND-THE-WORLD ITINERARY. WITH 45 DATES AROUND THE WORLD, SHAWN IS SURE TO BE VISITING A CITY NEAR YOU.

With World Tour rehearsals, award shows, album promo, modelling shoots and keeping his social media updated, Shawn's life is currently organized chaos. Having come a long way since buying his first ever album – Shania Twain's *Come On Over* – Shawn is now entering the most gruelling part of his career: the touring cycle. However, he has a simple pop philosophy to ensure he can handle life on the road. "The way I keep myself

Above Posing for selfies with fans outside *Good Morning America*, April 17, 2015.

Opposite One man and his army: Minnesota brings the noise! December 7, 2015.

sane is by thinking of it as fun," he said.

Prior to the release of *The Shawn Mendes EP* in 2014 and signing to Island Records, Shawn toured many cities of North America as a member of the MAGCON Tour. If you don't already know, the MAGCON (Meet and Greet Convention) family includes artists such as Nash Grier, Cameron Dallas, Matt Espinosa, Taylor Caniff, Aaron Carpenter, Carter Reynolds, Jack Johnson and Jack Gilinsky – a group of boys aged 15 to 19 who are blowing up on social media. Many of the stars are "Vine Famous", and the MAGCON tour provides the perfect opportunity for them to meet their thousands of fans.

Before the MAGCON family tour whisked Shawn away from his real family, Shawn played his first ever concert on October 26, 2013. "First time I played to an audience was this random day in Toronto where a couple people from Vine were going to meet their fans," he recalled. "That's when everything went from something impossible to a very tangible dream."

During all of Shawn's previous tours – ShawnsFirstHeadline and Shawn Mendes World Tour – as well as the Live on Tour with Austin Mahone and even as Taylor Swift's support act for her 1989 tour, there has been one consistent factor at every show: the cries of "We want Shawn! We want Shawn!" from the crowd. But now, out on his own massive world tour, these cries and screams are even more deafening, prompting Shawn to shout, "I cannot hear myself at all right now. I love that so much." It was during his now-famous Madison Square Garden show (sold out in five minutes) on September 10, 2016, that Shawn realised he had become a major star. "Standing on stage at Madison Square Garden was one of those moments when I knew I had made it. Just looking around like 'Woah, this is real', and seeing so many people there for me. It was surreal and crazy!"

With the rest of the world waiting in anticipation to see Shawn

"JUST THE FACT THAT A THOUSAND PEOPLE IN FRONT OF ME WERE READY TO HEAR ME SING WAS ONE OF THE BEST FEELINGS I CAN THINK OF." *SHAWN MENDES*

Opposite Shawn arrives with a smile at the Republic Records GRAMMY Celebration, February 15, 2016.

Below Performing 'Tiny Dancer' with Elton John at the Wiltern in Los Angeles, January 13, 2016.

up close and personal, the Illuminate World Tour promises to be a truly amazing spectacular. "I'm really excited to go everywhere," Shawn revealed about the tour to end all tours. "There are so many faraway places I haven't gone yet that I am finally going to get to." With his backstage rider complete with "oatmeal cereal crisps", his favourite pre-gig snack, Shawn is excited to unleash his latest music live and loud to his adoring fans.

"The tour is going to be amazing because we've practised so hard, but when the tour starts that will be the real show. I've never felt something change so rapidly in my life. From doing an entire acoustic set, to having a band all of sudden, to the production being involved. The set has just transformed like crazy. Right now, I start off acoustic and it goes into this beautiful, beautiful band section. It's just true, real live music... I like to think of it as an experience and less of a show."

For Shawn, playing music live is how he can intimately connect with his fans, and a heart-stopping show full of wonder, love and hard work is what his fans should always come to expect from him. "We've practised so much," he said in a recent interview. "But I'm never going to feel good enough, but I'm going do the best I can because that's all I've been doing. I'm just going go out there and have fun and connect with the crowd and do what I always do."

With 45 shows in total, the Illuminate World Tour will push Shawn and his band to the very limits of exhaustion. However, being the sensible and considerate boy he is, he'll take it all in his stride. "I'm very extreme about caring for my voice. Did people care about how a singer sounded live back in the day? I don't really feel like they did. Not everything was being filmed. Today, one huge mess-up and millions are seeing it. There's a lot more on the line nowadays. We're so cautious and scared of messing up. It adds a lot of stress to a career." Let's hope that Shawn's excitement, stress and nervousness doesn't get the better of him... again!

"I've had a few embarrassing experiences on stage," he has admitted. "One particular one was forgetting what city I was in, and shouting out the wrong city. That is the worst! Sometimes your brain just goes on you on stage and it's so embarrassing!"

Is Shawn on his way to your neighbourhood any time soon? Check shawnmendes.com for 2017 tour dates and get your ticket now!

This page Shawn plays it cool at SiriusXM Studio, June 3, 2016.

Opposite above Shawn Mendes goes electric at the Rays of Sunshine charity concert, Wembley Arena, London, October 24, 2016.

Opposite below Shawn Mendes and Hailee Steinfeld perform 'Stitches' at iHeartRadio's Music Festival, September 19, 2015.

ON THE MENDES

ONE LOOK AT SHAWN MENDES'S SOCIAL MEDIA AND YOU
CAN TELL THAT THE WORKAHOLIC HARDLY EVER TAKES A DAY
OFF TO HEAL AND RELAX, NO MATTER HOW WELL DESERVED IT
MAY BE. HOWEVER, ON THE ODD DAY OFF BETWEEN TOURING
THE WORLD AND RELEASING NO. 1 ALBUMS, SHAWN TAKES
HIS ME TIME VERY SERIOUSLY, AND IT'S SOMETHING HE ASKS
HIS FANS TO RESPECT.

"Just turning your phone off," the songwriter admits is step one to
feeling relaxed. "You just have to sometimes. You got to know when
to turn it off and go back to reality for a minute."

It is when Shawn is "back in reality" on his day off that he can
truly turn off from his day job.

Shawn's idol is the guitarist and songwriter John Mayer, who was
a major influence during the recording of *Illuminate* ("I think John
inspired the album more than anybody"). And it was Mayer who
encouraged – *insisted* – that Shawn work hard but also play hard.
"John Mayer said, 'It's OK to take time off. It's OK to go through
stages of highs and lows – that just teaches you and makes you grow
as a person.'" "That helped me," Shawn admitted.

The highs of the screaming fans, and the lows of lonely tour
buses and a blur of blink-and-you-miss-it hotel rooms, can leave
bright new stars feeling on the edge of a supernova implosion.
How on earth does Shawn like to relax and unwind? "I like to work
out a lot, me and my friends and crew on the road. And also just
relax, if we're somewhere warm go to a pool, or beach," he has said.
When Shawn and his band are not somewhere warm, they take
their exhausted feet for a walk... to their nearest pedicure salon! In
July 2016, Shawn famously tweeted: "Today I got a pedicure and
the lady told me I was in the top three of longest toe hair she'd ever
seen. She's been doing it for 10 years." The tweet was read around
the world, and even made it to the front page of several online pop
news pages – much to Shawn's horror, toe doubt!

Toe hair aside, what Shawn savours the most about taking time
off is the freedom to go wherever he likes. "Truthfully, I don't
think there will ever be a time when I can't walk across the street
to go to a restaurant. It's up to you to keep your life as normal as
possible," he has said recently. Of course, all that might change
after performing to more than a million new fans on the Illuminate
World Tour, but Shawn is serious about having fun on his own
time, away from the bright spotlights of fame. "I will forever have
time to take photos with fans and talk to them if they want to talk,"
Shawn said in a recent interview. "But when it comes to having
time to myself, I take it seriously. You can't give the world your

AND THE WINNER IS...

2014 TEEN CHOICE AWARDS
Choice Web Star: Music

2014 SHORTY AWARDS
Vine Musician

2014 MUCH MUSIC VIDEO AWARDS
Fan Fave Video, "Something Big"

2015 STREAMY AWARDS
Breakthrough Artist

2015 MTV EUROPE MUSIC AWARDS
Best New Artist

2016 PEOPLE'S CHOICE AWARDS
Favourite Breakout Artist

2016 NICKELODEON KIDS' CHOICE AWARDS
Favourite New Artist

2016 MUCH MUCH VIDEO AWARDS
Video of the Year, "I Know What You Did Last Summer"

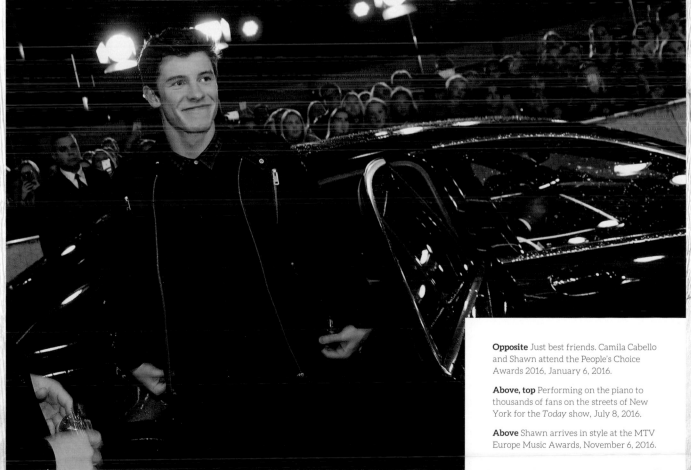

Opposite Just best friends. Camila Cabello and Shawn attend the People's Choice Awards 2016, January 6, 2016.

Above, top Performing on the piano to thousands of fans on the streets of New York for the *Today* show, July 8, 2016.

Above Shawn arrives in style at the MTV Europe Music Awards, November 6, 2016.

"I'LL NEVER FEEL LIKE I'VE MADE IT. YOU CAN'T GET TOO COMFORTABLE AND RELAX BECAUSE YOUR WORLD CAN FLIP OVERNIGHT. THERE HAVE BEEN ARTISTS WHO'VE SOLD OUT ARENAS ONE YEAR, AND THE NEXT THEY CAN'T FILL A THEATRE. THERE'S ALWAYS MORE TO ACHIEVE." *SHAWN MENDES*

This page The Vine star found fame uploading songs from his bedroom, while playing guitar on his bed.

Opposite The gig that changed everything: Shawn's famous Madison Square Garden show, September 10, 2016.

whole self, or you'd fall apart. I give as much as I can, and then I have to take time for myself."

A self-proclaimed "very average guy", Shawn has learned that the music industry can at times be a lonely and difficult place, where his superstar career can make it difficult to meet real and sincere people – including a girlfriend, obviously. "It's hard to connect with people when you work in this industry," he said in a recent interview. "Even though I'm not an intimidating person, my career is. People will automatically think, 'Oh, he's a douchebag because he's famous', and they'll be mean. But if they took the time to get to know me, then they'd understand I'm not that person. I'm very down-to-earth."

While it is Shawn's earnest, polite and people-pleasing personality and small-town charm that has helped him win over the entire world, it is also what keeps him up at night. To us, Shawn is the perfect pop package, a true Mr Nice Guy. For Shawn, he is racked with anxiety to make sure he never disappoints his fans, and that his dreams continue to come true. "It's hard for me to just say, 'Wow, this is amazing – I'm famous. I'm living the dream!'," he admitted in an interview. "I sit there and think, I'm scared – this can go away tomorrow. My biggest fear is that one day, not as many people show up or, one day, not as many people favourite a tweet. Which is funny to say, but it's true."

Suffice to say, for now, the Mendes Army are here to stay, here to listen and here to "favourite" what Shawn has to say. Because the Mendes Army are a loyal bunch – aren't we?

THE MENDES ARMY

YOU KNOW YOU'VE HIT THE BIG TIME WHEN FANS START CALLING THEMSELVES BY A COLLECTIVE TERM. ED HAS HIS SHEERIOS. 5 SECONDS OF SUMMER HAVE THEIR 5SOS FAM. JUSTIN HAS HIS BELOVED BELIEBERS. FOR SHAWN, HIS MILLIONS OF FANS ARE KNOWN SIMPLY AS THE MENDES ARMY – AND THEY COULD CONQUER THE WORLD WITH THEIR LOVE!

Over the past three years, Shawn's fans have had the opportunity to grow up with their idol. In that time, the singer-songwriter has also grown up, grown wise and grown to understand that he would just be "a normal kid in Toronto" without his fans. "From 15 to 18, I feel like I'm a whole different person," Shawn stated in a recent interview. "I think my understanding of the world has changed. My patience has grown because of my understanding,

and being able to grasp life and not let it get to me too much."

In those three years, Shawn has released two world-class albums and travelled the globe on a sold-out arena world tour in 2016 and the Illuminate World Tour in 2017. He witnessed Taylormania first-hand while on tour with Ms Swift's 1989 stadium spectacular, and the series of intense performances he gave was a steep learning curve for the young artist. He also discovered just how loved he is

"I'M SO GRATEFUL TO HAVE A CONNECTION LIKE I DO WITH YOU GUYS." *SHAWN MENDES*

by his fans. "I am the luckiest person in the world," he has enthused. "Human interaction is the biggest thing." He also said, "I'm so grateful to have a connection like I do with my fans." And Shawn means it. "Once, I signed 900 autographs. In one night!," he proudly claims.

With his fame arising from social media, Shawn is keen to give back. That's the reason the young singer has launched his #NotesFromShawn campaign via DoSomething.org, and why he often tweets to thank his fans for their dedicated and often unbelievable devotion. "It's easy to be creative and push the boundaries of life when you have the most supportive fans in the world. Guys, thank you," he posted to Twitter in October 2016.

With the 18-year-old topping the charts around the world, it's anyone's guess where the singer goes from here. His 2017 World Tour will see him perform to more than a million members of the Mendes Army, no doubt picking up even more fans along the way. But how does Shawn cope with all his fan attention? He has a simple technique: "I just tell them 'Calm down, I'm just a regular person'. I

think fans forget that sometimes when they see me on the internet and in pictures. When they see me in person they kind of explode because it's almost like, 'No way! He's a real person', and I'll say, 'I'm real, I'm just like you'. When I say that they kind of calm down immediately."

As the Mendes Army gets bigger, and louder, and as Shawn's star shines ever brighter, the singer is adamant that fame and fortune will not change him. He's too down to earth, too grounded by his family and close friends from home to become a "douchebag", as he called it.

"I want people keeping things normal and not treating me any differently. The worst thing would be for people to start treating me like a king, because then you start to believe you are one." Besides, Shawn loves his fans way too much to ever become disconnected from them, or aloof. He's not the arrogant type. Shawn's sincere love and admiration of his fans is one more reason why this performer from Pickering has become the most adored artist on the planet. "One of the biggest things is staying in contact with my fans – very intimate contact," he teased. Lucky us!

"SHAWN'S FANS ARE A REFLECTION OF HIM; HE'S A REALLY NICE GUY." *CAMILA CABELLO*

Opposite Shawn gets Pitbull's Revolution 2016 New Year's Eve party started!

Above top Lisbon loves Shawn! Portuguese Fans show Shawn signs of affection, May 8, 2016.

Above Mendes selfie madness with fans at the MTV Europe Music Awards, November 6, 2016.

MENDES MANIA

MUSIC'S "FIRST VINE STAR" HAS COME A VERY LONG WAY IN A VERY SHORT TIME. FROM PICKERING IN ONTARIO TO PICKING UP LOADS OF WORLD MUSIC AWARDS, MENDES IS FILLING THE HEARTS OF POP FANS WITH LOVE AND JOY AS MENDES MANIA SWEEPS THE WORLD.

This page Shawn accepts the award for Favorite Breakout Artist, People's Choice Awards 2016, January 6, 2016.

Opposite A pop-up show on top of the marquee at Radio City Music Hall – what a gig! October 22, 2015.

"When did this happen?" Shawn recently exclaimed in an interview. "When did this many people know who I was? I love it! The fact that that many people gravitate toward my music is really cool." With an ever-growing contacts list on his iPhone, Shawn has become the hottest star on planet Earth. His manager, Andrew Gertler, believes this is all due to his "one-to-one relationship" with his fans. "It really does come down to him as a person," Andrew says of Shawn's charm. "What's amazing is that from the day that I met him as a 15-year-old to now, with the increasing success, is that what drives him as a person hasn't changed for a second. He does a good job of surrounding himself with great people and also of keeping himself in the right mindset." Shawn's ability to recognize the good in others has helped him build a great network of friends, family and fans to keep him grounded while the rest of the world has Mendes mania.

While this hype and hysteria would make most 18-year-olds go crazy – just look at Mr Bieber when he was 18! – Shawn had learned from his peer's mistakes and is learning to take all his fame and fortune one day at a time. "Even at this point, I don't feel like

I'm caught up talent-wise to my career," he said. "There is such a hype and a big build-up to me, and it's very hard to meet those expectations. That's been a big stress in my life. I never felt like I was good enough and, only nowadays, am I starting to feel like I deserve all this. I felt like there were so many talented people who should be getting what I have." Shawn has admitted that he had to learn "six times faster than average" in order to keep up and process being thrust into fame: "Right now, I can't be like, 'Oh my God, I just sold out Radio City. I'm the shit. I'm so cool.' What if next week no one knows who I am?"

While Shawn has a long list of admirers, from Camila Cabello to Hailee Steinfeld, Justin Bieber to Ed Sheeran, and even his idol, John Mayer, the singer is still trying his best to take it all one step at a time. "I'm still changing and learning [about] my fans as they are learning [about] me as a person. As one person it takes time for the world to understand you just as you have to understand them." We think Shawn's doing a great job!

Not surprisingly, all of Shawn's fame and wealth has meant putting a barrier up around his heart, and his fame has negatively impacted on his ability to find a long-term girlfriend. Meeting girls is hard, he admits: "It's hard to get through that first bubble, not just with girls but with everyone. It's not that I can't connect, it just takes a little more effort. I almost have to make myself completely vulnerable for people to feel comfortable around me. I don't get upset about it, I just have to work round it because that's my life now." However, single life isn't too hard for the handsome singer: "I really like funny girls, girls with a witty sense of humour; so if someone is able to catch on to what I'm saying very quickly, I find that very attractive. I also really like brunettes... and also, dancers! I have a thing for dancers!"

If you want to keep up with Shawn, you better put your dancing shoes on...

"CUTE GIRLS TAKING PICTURES OF ME ALL THE TIME; WHY WOULD I EVER GET ANNOYED?" *SHAWN MENDES*

This page When Shawn met James – it got a bit silly! *The Late Late Show with James Corden*, September 28, 2016.

Opposite above In honour of Elton, Shawn and the Rocket Man go perform together. A unique treat.

Opposite below London's Apollo lit up by Shawn on May 5, 2016.

On November 7, 2015, Shawn received the Allan Slaight Honour at Canada's Walk of Fame ceremony in Toronto. This award recognizes "Vine's first star" as a young inspirational Canadian musician who has achieved international success. Hollywood – you're next!

"I'LL NEVER FORGET THAT FEELING WHEN YOU WALK OUT IN FRONT OF A CROWD THAT YOU KNOW IS ALL THERE FOR YOU. IT IS SO UNREAL" *SHAWN MENDES*

Shawn wows the *Billboard* Music Awards with a solo piano performance, May 22, 2016.

LIFE OF THE PARTY

A NO. 1 EP, TWO NO. 1 ALBUMS, THREE WORLD TOURS, MILLIONS OF MEMBERS OF THE MENDES ARMY – ALL ACHIEVED BY HIS NINETEENTH BIRTHDAY. WHAT ON EARTH WILL SHAWN DO NEXT? WE HAVE NO IDEA. BUT ONE THING IS FOR SURE – IT'LL BE AWESOME.

"I feel I'm a lot older than my age," said Shawn in a recent interview, not unsurprisingly with all that he has already accomplished. "I've been working straight for three years." Nobody owns a crystal ball to look into the future of the multitalented musician, but anything that Shawn puts his mind to he will achieve.

"I'd love to go to university one day, if I get a chance," Shawn said. "I'd like to study guitar." For Shawn, success is "doing what you love for a living", and the singer has expressed much interest in pursuing his love of acting at some point in his future. "As soon as I get time, I really want to dig down and do some acting," he stated. His favourite role? "Spider-Man? I'm kidding. Anything, really. I love acting. It doesn't matter what it is. In the music videos we're releasing you get to see the acting. I would love to go and venture into that land." It's fascinating to think that one day, we'll see Shawn up on the big screen, putting as much passion into talking for a living as he does singing.

This decision to act, as well as write and perform songs, perfectly encapsulates the very essence of who Shawn is. Despite what he says(!), he is not your average pop star – who takes the money and runs. Shawn defies expectations and perceptions, he raises his own game – he surprises people with his anxieties and ambitions. He's not a pop puppet.

Shawn's biggest fear is that nobody will turn up at a gig, but we, his fans, know that's unlikely. The reason he has become such a massive star is that we need someone who isn't just after the 15 minutes of fame and the 15 million dollars. Shawn isn't manufactured. He's not a fake reality TV star. *He's real*. And so is his desire to entertain the world. Andrew Gertler agrees: "I think the biggest challenge has been showing the world that Shawn is more than a teenage artist. People are expecting a teen artist to make a certain kind of music, and Shawn wants to make great songwriter music. Even in people's minds and perceptions, they're like, 'He's a teenager so he can't do that.'"

Changing people's perceptions of his music and positive personality, and spreading joy is something Shawn is passionate about and deeply committed to. Shawn wants to use the power of his music to empower the minds and hearts of his fans. In summer 2016, Shawn partnered with Paper Mate InkJoy Gel Pens to help the Spread Joy, Not Smears campaign. The campaign is designed to help fans share handwritten notes with each other to encourage positivity and boost self-esteem as part of Shawn's awesome #NotesFromShawn campaign with DoSomething.org. However, you get the feeling from Shawn that even without the fame or the wealth that his songwriting brings, he would still be waking up

"YOU LOOK BACK AT PEOPLE LIKE ELVIS AND THE BEATLES AND STILL GET THEIR MUSIC BECAUSE IT'S TIMELESS. THAT'S WHAT I WANT."

SHAWN MENDES

every morning and injecting positivity into the world, regardless of whether anyone was watching. His celebrity only amplifies how much good he can do.

"I just try to be as much as the same I would be if this wasn't happening," Shawn revealed about his increasing fame. "I'm just living and doing what makes me happy. If it makes me happy to go home and see my friends and family, then I go home and see my friends and family. If it makes me happy to be working my ass off for a month straight, then I work my ass off for a month straight. I vow to myself that I'm just going to do whatever it takes to make myself happy, without, obviously, affecting other people's lives in a bad way."

And that, in a nutshell, is why we love you, Shawn. It's a crazy world out there, but we can all take comfort in the fact that there is a caring, genuine, talented popstar that we can believe in: his name is Shawn Mendes.

SHAWN'S BEST COVERS: TOP 10

Which track is your favourite?

1. 'SAY SOMETHING'
2. 'FAKE LOVE'
3. 'DRAG ME DOWN'
4. 'SUMMERTIME SADNESS'
5. 'SHE LOOKS SO PERFECT'
6. 'HALLELUJAH'
7. 'HELLO'
8. 'SKINNY LOVE'
9. 'HOTLINE BLING'
10. 'COUNTING STARS'

Lights! Camera! Shawn! The singer storms the American Music Awards, November 20, 2016.